Using Language

Helen Astley and
Eric Hawkins

This book looks at the different things we do with words and at how our use of language depends on

· who we are · who we are talking or writing to · what they know already · what we think we are expected to say

The book has six units

1. **A day in the life of a language user**

2. **Words at work**

3. **Language for the fun of it!**

4. **Who are you?**

5. **Who are you talking to or writing to?**

6. **Bad language**

The right of the University of Cambridge to print and sell all manner of books was granted by Henry VIII in 1534. The University has printed and published continuously since 1584.

CAMBRIDGE UNIVERSITY PRESS

Cambridge

New York   New Rochelle

Melbourne   Sydney

1 A day in the life of a language user

Chart your day

How much of your day is spent in using language?
How much time do you spend doing other things, such as eating and sleeping?
(Perhaps language overlaps with your meals, and in your dreams.)

S

Try to work out roughly how you spend the next 24 hours beginning at school tomorrow morning and finishing at the same time the next day.

1. Make an activities chart to show how much time is spent on the following:

sleeping	talking
listening to others	listening to the radio (or a cassette)
watching TV	writing
eating	playing

(and any other ways you spend your time)
You will probably have to keep a note each hour of the day and evening. You won't be able to measure it to the minute. If two activities overlap (such as eating and talking, or eating and watching TV), decide which activity is most important and count that. If they are equally important, divide the time in half.

2. Work out *very roughly* how long you spend on each activity and arrange them in order. You may like to arrange them on a 'bar graph'. (Your graph may not look exactly like the one on page 3! It is only an example.)

3. Which of your activities involved language? Mark them with an 'L'.

Are the times for your activities the same as those of the rest of your class?

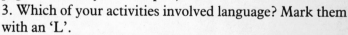

G

Work out the average time spent by your class on the most common activities.

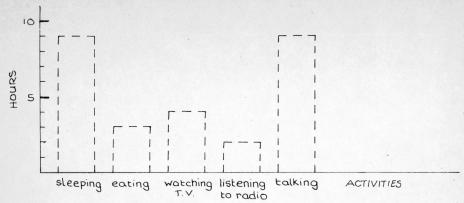

Although animals don't use language as we do, they can give quite complicated messages to each other. These are mostly concerned with getting food, mating, warning of danger – the difficult business of just staying alive. The messages that humans send each other can also be about things like this, but humans lead more complicated lives than animals. We send and receive messages of many different kinds.

You will have sent and received many messages yourself
[S] today. Try to make a list of some of them, setting them out like the ones below.

Time	Sender	Receiver	Message	Result (if any)	Kind of message
7:30	my mum	me	'Get up!'	I stayed in bed!	order
8:00	my French penfriend	me	(postcard) 'J'arrive à Londres le 28 juillet.'	I showed it to my mum	information
8:30	me	my friend	'Hi!'	my friend said 'hello'	greeting
9:45	my friend	me	'Are you going swimming tonight?'	I said 'yes'	question
10:45	my teacher	me	'You won't find the answer by looking out of the window'	I looked at my book	telling off!

Are the messages received from teachers mostly of one kind?
What messages are usually received from parents/friends?

Get the message?

Here are the spoken messages exchanged by one family as they got up and came down for breakfast:

1. Do you know what time it is?
2. I *am* getting up!
3. I can't find my socks!
4. Cornflakes please!
5. Ta dad!
6. Thank goodness it's Friday!
7. Have you seen my trainers?
8. No, why should I?
9. What do you mean, I haven't combed my hair?
10. Try taking the top off first!
11. Well done!
12. Bye mum!
13. Be careful!
14. O.K. Don't worry!
15. What a lousy day!
16. Somebody's left the door open!

Each of these speakers was trying to do something with words.

Below is a list of some of the things we do with language. Try to find an example of each in the family's spoken messages. Example: *Asking for information*: Do you know what time it is?

(a) asking (i) for information (asking a question)
(ii) for something or asking someone to do something (making a request)
(b) telling (giving information)
(c) refusing (to do or say something)
(d) advising (warning or threatening or persuading or suggesting? What is the difference between these uses of language?)
(e) ordering
(f) promising

(g) greeting
(h) thanking
(i) denying (saying something is not true or hasn't happened)
(j) showing friendship
(k) congratulating
(l) saying how you feel

1. Which of these ways of using language is the most common, do you think?

2. Which do you yourself use most often? And which least often? Discuss in your group which is the most/least common for all of you.

Talking and listening

Here is a list of some school lessons. Discuss in your group and say in which of these lessons you do most *talking* and in which you spend most time *listening*:

· English
· French, Spanish or German
· Science

· History
· P.E.
· Music

You have probably been told off more than once for 'talking in class'. Is talking in class always a bad thing? When might it be bad and when might it be good?

If you were a teacher would you let the children in your class talk whenever they wanted to?

Listening isn't easy!

If you don't understand what you are reading you can always go back and read it again. But you can't when you are listening to somebody. When somebody is explaining something to you it often helps you to have a picture or diagram to look at. At school what subjects are best learnt in this way?

Language for learning

Here are some of the ways in which things are learnt in sch

(a) listening to the teacher
(b) listening to radio or watching TV in class
(c) discussing with the teacher
(d) asking questions
(e) answering questions
(f) talking in a small group
(g) working in pairs
(h) reading on your own
(i) making your own notes
(j) writing or learning after the lesson (homework)
(k) learning by working with your hands

G
1. Can you suggest other ways of learning?
2. Which way of learning do you use most often?
3. Which do you find most useful?
4. Does your choice of the best way of learning depend on what you have to learn?
5. Choose your favourite subject and say, if you were the teacher, how you would like to help your pupils to learn it.

Hidden meanings

Look back at the things the family said in the morning (page 4). One of the remarks was: 'Somebody's left the door open!' On the *surface* this is a statement giving information (like (b) on our list, page 4.). But, *hidden* behind the statement is a request (like (a) (ii) on our list) or even an order (like (e) on our list) to 'Shut the door!' In the same way, when the playground bully says, 'Do you want a thick ear?' you know that it isn't a *question* but a *threat*.

S
What do you think are the *hidden* meanings underneath these surface meanings?
1. 'Your pudding is getting cold.' (said by one of your parents to you at dinner)
2. 'There's an awful draught from that window.' (said by person in coach)
3. 'I'm looking for Browning Avenue.' (said by lorry driver to passer-by)
Can you think of other examples?
We mostly guess hidden meanings from what we know about the speaker and from what we *expect* the speaker to say.

2 Words at work

Here are some of the things said by a man at work one morning. Can you work out what his job is and who he is talking to?

Morning! Keeping well?

Come in out of the rain. Filthy weather!

Yes! Fresh in this morning.

They're cheaper again this week

Ninety and one-forty and the bananas seventy that's just three pounds

Anything else Mrs Hawkins?

Look back at the kinds of messages on pages 4 and 5. You can find examples there of some of the things that this greengrocer does with words. For example:

telling (giving information): 'Fresh in this morning.'

G Can you find examples of
asking for information
advising (persuading)
greeting (just being friendly)

He also uses language in a way that was not listed on pages 4, 5. When he adds up figures he mutters the numbers to himself, so he is using language *to help himself to think*. He can also use language to help himself *to remember*, for example by writing a list of things to buy the next day in the market. And later he might want *to check* the list to make sure that he had got everything.

P Make up a conversation in a shop (any kind of shop – perhaps a clothes shop or a record shop), and work out what kinds of messages are being exchanged by those who speak. (Look again at the list on pages 4 and 5.)

Here is a list of people who use words in different ways:
- shopkeeper
- teacher
- parent (caring for young baby)
- disc jockey (on local radio station)
- auctioneer
- audio-typist
- actor/actress
- nurse
- school pupil (aged 12)

S Which of these people is likely to do
(a) most writing/least writing?   (b) most talking/least talking?

Draw a chart like ours and arrange these language users in 4 columns to show who does MOST/LEAST of TALKING/ LISTENING/WRITING/READING in their daily jobs. We've filled in six language users in the TALKING column and two in the LISTENING column. Do you agree with the order given? Rearrange them on your chart if you wish, and finish filling in the chart.

	TALKING	LISTENING	WRITING	READING
MOST	actor/actress	audio-typist		
	teacher			
	disc jockey			
	school pupil			
	nurse			
LEAST	audio-typist	auctioneer		

Thinking

We know the answer to easy sums (2 + 2) without having to say the words to ourselves. To work out more difficult ones, though, most of us need to say the numbers as we work them out. As we saw with the greengrocer, we even do this out loud. Try working out 90p + £1.40 + 70p without saying the numbers to yourself and you'll see how hard it is.

Language helps us to think in other ways. For example, if you are in trouble at school and know you will have to explain it to your parents, you probably run over in your mind what you

will say and what you think your parents will say. You think the problem out by putting it into words in your head.

Suggest some ways in which the following people might have to think beforehand of the words that *they* and *others are going to use*:

1. a teacher preparing a lesson
2. a parent who has to explain to a small child that the family cat has been run over
3. the presenter of a TV game show
4. someone about to ask the boss for an afternoon off
5. a child asking for an expensive bike for his or her birthday
6. a parent who has to explain that there is no money for a holiday this year

Talking things over helps us to get our ideas clear. Can you say how and think of any examples?

Checking and listing

Before a pilot takes off in an aircraft he or she runs through a 'checklist' of things that must be in order (fuel, oil pressure, ailerons, rudder etc.).
This is to prevent something being forgotten. Can you think of times when you or your family use checklists to make sure you haven't forgotten anything?

G Imagine you are going away for a week with a school group. Make a list of things you must pack, in only one suitcase. Compare your list with others in your group and check items you have forgotten.

Language has been used for making lists of things ever since writing was invented. Some of the earliest examples of ancient writings that have been discovered are lists of army equipment, stores of food etc. People who study ancient civilisations can use these lists to help them to decipher the old writing.

G We still use language to make lists. Think of the lists used in school, in a club you belong to, in shops and businesses.

Instructing

Language is used for giving instructions in several ways, for example:

1. Laws passed by Parliament, or bye-laws agreed by local authorities
2. Rules for playing games or for membership of a club

9

3. Instructions telling how to make things
4. Instructions telling how to do things
Here are some examples:

1. Extract from *The Highway Code*

Extra rules for cyclists

130 Before starting to ride, always look round and make sure that it is safe to move away from the kerb. Before turning right or left, moving out to pass or pulling up at the kerb, always glance behind and make sure it is safe. Give a clear arm signal to show what you intend to do.

2. Rules for playing *Scrabble*

8. Any words found in a standard dictionary are permitted except those starting with a capital letter, those designated as foreign words, abbreviations and words requiring apostrophes or hyphens. Consult a dictionary only to check spelling or usage. Any word may be challenged before the next player starts his turn. If the word challenged is unacceptable, the player takes back his tiles and loses his turn.

3. Recipe

Baked Bananas

Lay peeled bananas in a fireproof dish. Sprinkle with grated coconut, lemon juice and brown sugar. Dot with a little butter. Bake for 20 minutes in a hot oven (200°C). Serve warm with ice cream.

4. Extract from *St John Ambulance* manual – the 'Kiss of Life'

MOUTH-TO-MOUTH/NOSE VENTILATION

If casualty does not start to breathe after ensuring open airway, keep head tilted back and begin mouth-to-mouth/nose ventilation. This is easier to do when the casualty is lying on his back, but should be started whatever position the casualty happens to be in.

a. Open your mouth wide and take a deep breath.
b. Pinch the casualty's nostrils together.
c. Seal your lips around his mouth.
d. Blow into his lungs until the chest rises.

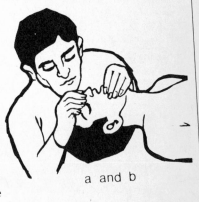

a and b

Choose one of these examples and say why it is important for the language to be clearly written and *unambiguous* (unambiguous = having only one possible meaning).

Persuading

Every day you will come across language being used to persuade you to do something (no, not just the washing up!). This is the language of advertising. Adverts will try to persuade you to buy something new, or choose one kind of chocolate rather than another, or even to vote for a particular political party.

G Watch some advertisements for washing powders on TV. Note down what seem to you to be the most important words used to persuade the viewer. Compare your list of words with those noted by the rest of the class. What are the commonest words used to advertise washing powders? Why do you think these words are chosen?

What are the commonest words used when advertising the following? · beer · pain killers (e.g. for headaches) · pipe tobacco★ · toilet rolls · instant coffee
★Why are cigarettes not advertised on TV now?

G There are many ways of making a message more persuasive. In a TV advert, for example, the scene will be carefully set, actresses/actors will have been specially chosen for the way they look and talk; cuddly pets and little children are popular because everybody likes them. Can you find examples?

Humour and catch phrases are used to strengthen the message. Find some examples.

Music is used in two ways:
(a) as background music to create an atmosphere
(b) in tuneful jingles that stay in the head
Can you find examples from your study of the TV programmes or advertisements?

Do you think the language of advertising is sometimes dishonest?
We will return to this when we consider 'loaded words' in Unit 6.

Slogans

Another way in which language guides our actions or opinions (perhaps without our realising it) is through slogans. Radio and television can quickly make a slogan popular. An example (before seat belts were compulsory) was: 'Clunk, click every trip!' What did this remind us to do? Do you think this slogan really worked?

Here are some other slogans that have been used:

CARELESS TALK
COSTS LIVES

Go
smash
an egg

G Can you find out what each of these tried to make people do?

Make a list of some of the slogans used today by the Government, by political parties and by advertisers.
Do you think they are effective? Try to say exactly how they work on people.
Can a slogan ever stop us from thinking for ourselves?

P Discuss in your group a change that you would like to see, in school or outside. Then work in pairs to invent a slogan to make the idea popular.

Do's and don'ts

G On your next journey to school make a list of the different notices that tell people what to do. Compare your list with your group and make a display of the different kinds of *instructions* we meet in the street.
What kinds of things are people told NOT to do?
Are some instructions more strongly stated than others? Try to find instructions that use strong language and some that put their message more gently. Which do you think has more effect on you? How does the LENGTH of an instruction affect its message?

BICYCLES
MUST NOT BE LEFT
IN THIS ARCHWAY

DEPOSITING
OF RUBBISH
STRICTLY
PROHIBITED

STRICTLY
NO PARKING
HOSPITAL ACCESS

FIRE EXIT
KEEP CLEAR

PLEASE
KEEP OFF
THE GRASS
DÉFENSE DE MARCHER
SUR LES PELOUSES

3 Language for the fun of it!

But life is not just to do with checking or persuading or do's and don'ts.

Language makes life more exciting, interesting, and often more fun.

Stories

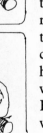

Think yourself back into a time when there was no radio, no TV, no electricity, no trains or motor cars, no sports clubs, no books . . . How do you think you would have spent the long, dark evenings round the fire?

It would be natural to tell stories to keep each other amused. Sometimes people passed a story round a circle – one person starting and the next carrying on. Sometimes there were professional storytellers and sometimes the storytellers sang their stories (the 'minstrels' of the Middle Ages). People remembered stories the way they were told and told them in turn to their own children. Sometimes the stories got a bit changed on the way, but all sorts of important ideas and historical events got passed on in this way, without anyone writing anything down.

Do you remember stories that your mother or father told you when you were small? Have you ever passed them on to a younger brother or sister?

Your grandparents probably remember stories from their own childhood. Try recording some of these on tape. You could ask them to tell you about a holiday when they were small perhaps or about their first job.

Then you could edit these and put the best ones together on one tape.

Feelings into words

· · · · · · · · · · · ·
· · · · · · · · · · · ·
· · **I'm bored!**

¡HATE!
YOU

I LOVE YOU

DON'T I KNOW

WHY I FEEL SAD

Fear

Curling fingers
crawling up
the back
of your
brain,
taking your mind
by
surprise,
then gripping
your heart and
squeezing it
of it's
life source.
A plunger
pushing
the contents
of your
stomach
down and
out

Deepak Kalha

We've probably all said some of the words above at some time. Sometimes just saying them, expressing them, makes you feel better (it may make someone else feel worse, of course!). The effect of putting feelings into words is very powerful. Why is that?

The feelings expressed in words in poetry are perhaps the most powerful of all. Read Deepak Kalha's poem 'Fear'.

Now think of any other poems you know that express feelings. Try to say which words make each poem especially effective for you.

Dear Diary

A diary is not usually meant to be read by anybody except the writer. Some people write their private thoughts to their diary as though to a friend. It can be written in a secret language. One famous diarist, Samuel Pepys (pronounced 'Peeps'), who lived through exciting times such as the Great Fire of London in 1666, and met many famous people, used a kind of shorthand with code words for the most private things he wrote about.

The final page of Pepys' diary.

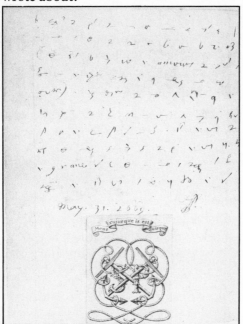

S Try as an experiment to keep a diary for a week. Write it up each night and say as truthfully as you can what you have seen, heard and thought during the day. Like Samuel Pepys you may want to invent your own shorthand or secret code for some of it. Is the writing in your diary different from most of the writing you do in school? If so, how and why?

Please write soon

1. How often do you write a letter? How often do you get one?
2. With modern inventions like the telephone do you think that letters are still necessary? Why and when are letters still needed?
3. Letters between friends have been called 'written conversation'. Do you think this is a good description? List the ways in which the language of a letter is different from conversation.

G

Songs

People sing songs for lots of reasons. In some parts of the world they sing to make the rain fall or to drive evil spirits away. Songs are also sung to wish people happiness, for instance when they get married. In the Middle Ages, stories – some made up, others about real happenings – were sung by travelling minstrels. The printing press was invented in 1440, and from the sixteenth to the nineteenth century the songs were printed in enormous numbers and sold by 'ballad mongers' (see left).

1. People still make songs to tell stories. Find examples of modern songs that tell stories.
2. Think of songs connected with sport which try to make things happen, rather like spells to make the rain fall.

What is your favourite song at the moment? Would you like the song just as much if it had no words, just a tune?

Take a break

When you tell your friends jokes at school during break you are using language just for fun. And many playground rhymes use language for fun (skipping rhymes, for example). The counting-out at the beginning of a game is 'dipping' in many places. Here are some dips. What dips do you know?

1. Dip, dip, dip,
   My blue ship,
   Sailing on the water
   Like a cup and saucer.
   Dip, dip, dip,
   You are not *it*!

2. One potato, two potato
   Three potato, four –
   Five potato, six potato
   Seven potato more.

3. Near Keswick in the North of England, children use the 'shepherd's score' in their counting-out games:

yan (1)	pimp (5)	dothera (9)
tan (2)	sethera (6)	dick (10)
tethera (3)	lethera (7)	yan-dick (11)
methera (4)	hothera (8)	tan-dick (12) and so on

4. **German**: Ene, mene, mei,
   du bist frei
   ene, mene, Maus,
   du musst 'raus

5. **French:** Am stram gram
   Pic et pic et colégram
   Bour et bour et ratatam
   Am stram gram
   Pic!

Word-play

Many jokes are based on word-play (puns). They are usually
'groan' jokes. Try these:

These kinds of jokes go in and out of fashion – just like
clothes.

Tongue-twisters go on for ever:
The sixth Sheik's sixth sheep's sick.

So do riddles:

Q. Why is it impossible to starve in the desert?
A. Because of the sandwiches there.

G All languages play with words. Ask someone to translate this French riddle:

Q. C'est un condamné qu'on n'arrive pas à guillotiner, pourquoi?
A. Il n'est pas coupable.

1. Make a class collection of riddles and illustrate them all.
2. Find out from members of the class who speak other languages than English some riddles in their languages.
3. Of the 'groan' jokes listed on page 17, only the one about the clock tower could be translated into other languages. Why wouldn't the other ones make sense?

Word games
You probably know how to play these word games:
1. Twenty questions 2. Chain Whispers 3. Kim's Game
4. Charades 5. 'I packed my bag and in it I put . . .'
6. What's my Line?
Remember you can play these games in any language. Have you tried them in French or German or Spanish?
What other word games do you know? Can you think of any that are played on radio or television?
Some more suggestions:
7. Choose a long word like BIRMINGHAM and see how many words of at least 3 letters you can make from the letters of the word, in two minutes.
8. Made-up words. Two volunteers invent a word (e.g. GEEK) whose meaning only they know. They then hold a conversation in which they keep using the word in its correct meaning and the rest try to guess what it means.
9. Matching words to actions. The teacher gives instructions as in 'Simon Says' but they must only be obeyed by the class if the leader *does* exactly what he or she *says*.
10. Making up secret codes and exchanging messages.
G Now have a go at playing some of these games.

Who are you?

What's in a name?

When a child is born the parents must *register* the birth and get a Birth Certificate for their child.
Your Birth Certificate has at least two names: your family name and one or more 'given' or 'first' names.

Above is a Birth Certificate for someone called John SMITH. These are some of the names that people might call him:
John, Jack, Johnnie, Mr Smith, Smithy, Sir, mate, you, 'guv', Dad, Grandad, mister, Uncle John.
1. Can you think of any other names that he might be called?
2. Who would use each of these names when talking to John Smith?

S 1. Make a similar list of the names that people give to you. Do you always get the same name in school?
2. Do you have a nickname? (Originally an 'ekename'; 'eke' or

'ick' meant 'also' in Old English, so it was an 'extra name':
'an ickname' became 'a nickname'.)

3. Do you like your nickname? Can anyone use it?

4. Would you have preferred to have been called some other name by your parents?

5. We sometimes feel upset when people forget our name. Why, do you think?

6. If we want to insult someone we call them names. What is the worst name you can call anybody?

7. Some children find it hard to believe that adults (teachers for instance) have a first name. What name do you use when speaking to your parents?

8. Sometimes our first name is called a 'Christian name'. Why?

Fashions in names

Parents take great care over choosing first names for their children. Here are the three most popular names for children born in the years 1900, 1925, 1950 and 1975:

	1900		1925		1950		1975	
girls	boys	girls	boys	girls	boys	girls	boys
Florence	William	Joan	John	Susan	David	Claire	Stephen
Mary	John	Mary	William	Linda	John	Sarah	Mark
Alice	George	Joyce	George	Christine	Peter	Nicola	Paul

Can you see any reason for the popularity of some of these names? (Names of royalty? A famous pioneer of nursing?)

Make a chart of the names of members of your year in school showing which are most popular. If you have a micro in school you might be able to put together a program on this – possibly covering all the names in the school.

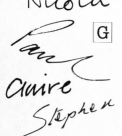

Where do first names come from?

Some of the commonest first names come from the Bible: Adam (meaning 'red'), Eve (meaning 'lively'); Sharon is a place in the Bible; Susan meant 'lily'. Many names come from Latin and Greek. Examples are: Diana (goddess of the moon); Martin (who came from Mars); Peter (the rock); Amanda (who deserved to be loved).

Names often become popular because of some famous person or even some character in a book. Can you think of some recent examples? Some names are in fashion and then go out of fashion. Sometimes names run in families. Think of the British Royal family – you can see the same names being used again and again through their history.

In Roman Catholic countries it is common for children to be given the name of the saint on whose 'saint's day' they happen to be born. Religious names are also common: Jesús; Concepción.

S To find the meanings of names you have to look in a *dictionary of names* in the library. See if you can find out what your first name meant originally. Find out from your parents if you were nearly called something else.

Family names

Many family names tell what job the holder of the name used to do. Examples are: Miller; Archer; Taylor.

It is the same in other languages: Schmidt, Boulanger. What did these people do?

Other names tell where people lived: Hill; East; Wood or Heim; Desmoulins; de los Ríos. Many names were originally nicknames describing a person's appearance: Short, Longfellow. Oher names originally meant 'son of' as in Johnson, Jackson. (This is something we share with the Scandinavian countries: Johansson; Erikson.) In Scots Gaelic language 'son of' is Mac or Mc, as in Macdonald. In Irish 'son of' is 'O', as in O'Brien.

S Here are some family names. Suggest where each one came from: Cooke; Blackwell; MacArthur; Strong; Shepherd; Smith; Müller; la Fontaine; del Mar; Fischer

In some parts of Wales, where there are lots of Joneses, they say 'Jones the post' or 'Jones the milk' so that they know which one is meant. In Denmark it used to be common (it is now a bit old-fashioned) to put people's jobs in front of their names: Jans Larsson who runs the chemist's shop would be called: 'Hr. Apoteker Larsson' (Mr Pharmacist Larsson).

Can you think of ways in which we show what people do by what we call them?

It's a mstery!

In English 'Mrs' is used for married women and 'Miss' for unmarried women. There is only one word, 'Mr', for men and this does not show whether or not they are married. Do you think this is a good idea? What would you think of calling all men 'Master' unless they were married?

Some women prefer to be called 'Ms'. Why? What do you think of this? In Britain, when women marry they usually take the family name of their husband (and so do their children), although they do not have to. What do you think of this?

You? Thou? Ye?

ON ILKLEY MOOR BAHT 'AT

TRADITIONAL

Early Nineteenth Century Tune

This folk song comes from Yorkshire. The line *Wheear 'as tha bin sin' ah saw thee?* ('Where hast thou been since I saw thee?') is in Yorkshire dialect. Many regional dialects have kept older forms of the language such as *thou* and its plural form *ye*. We can see older forms of language in the earlier translations of the Bible used by the Churches: e.g. 'Our Father, which *art* in Heaven, hallowed be *thy* name'; and 'O *ye* of little faith'. In the Yorkshire dialect *thou* or *tha* is used when speaking to one person and 'you' for more than one.

Most languages in Europe still show this difference between 'thou' and 'you'. So, in French, if you are speaking to more than one person, the word for 'you' is always *vous*. But if you are speaking to just one person you use either *tu* or *vous*. Which one you use depends on whom you are talking to or writing to. You use *tu* to your own friends and close family, but you use *vous* to be polite to older people and strangers.

TEACHER TO PUPIL: Tu n'es pas sage!
                  PUPIL: Mais vous . . . . .
                TEACHER: Tu vas te taire?

G Find out by asking members of your group and your teachers which languages have a 'thou' as well as a 'you', and if the difference is similar to the difference between the French *tu* and *vous*. Is English the odd one out here?

Talking 'proper'

The dialect of English that this book is written in is called 'standard English'. It became accepted as 'standard' because it was the dialect spoken in the capital (London), at court, in government, and at the universities. Then it was taken up by writers and printers throughout the country. But many different dialects exist. Each dialect has its own grammar rules.

Examples:

regional dialects		standard dialect
Yorkshire:	Wheear *as tha* bin? I *were* Don't jump off *while* the bus stops	Where *have you* been? I *was* Don't jump off *until* the bus stops
Devon:	I *be*	I *am*
Jamaican:	*me* can't	*I* can't
Suffolk:	*us* like	*we* like
Geordie:	*us* job	*our* job
Scottish:	*had you* a good time last night	*did you have* a good time . . .

Many American speakers of English will say 'I have *gotten* the message.' This is correct in 'standard American', and to say 'I have *got* the message' would be to break the rules.

G Discuss with your teacher the ways in which the words and rules of *your* local dialect are different from 'standard English'.

Often people speak the *dialect* of 'standard English' with their own local *accent*, so, although they are standard speakers, you can tell where they come from (e.g. Yorkshire, the West Country etc.). There is a difference, then, between dialect and accent. Can you say what the difference is?

If people can be understood clearly, does it matter what accent they have? In fact, people *do* seem to be more impressed by some accents than by others. Experiments have shown that we are all prejudiced about certain accents. That means that simply from the accent, without knowing the person, we may judge him or her to be: · stupid or clever · honest or dishonest · well-educated or ignorant, etc.

Talking 'posh'

For a long time news readers on radio and television had to have an accent which did not show the region from which they came. This accent is sometimes called 'BBC English' or 'RP' (received pronunciation). It is the accent which is associated with standard English.
1. Why do you think the BBC preferred this accent?
2. Is this changing now? Can you think of presenters on radio or television who do not use 'RP'?

Advertisers often use our prejudices about accents to their advantage. Listen to some advertisements and notice the different accents that are used. Sometimes a regional accent is used because it suggests 'straightforward, no-nonsense, common-sense'. Can you find examples in television advertisements?
A local product (e.g. cider) is sometimes associated, through the accent of the advertisement, with a particular region. Can you find examples?

1. What accent would you expect to find advertisers using to sell: wholemeal bread; painkillers; exotic perfumes; pet-foods; computer games; a set of encyclopaedias?
2. What is your favourite accent? Why do you like it? Is there an accent you don't like? Why not?
3. Are you happy with your own accent? How would you describe it?
4. Has anybody ever criticised your accent? Why?
5. Do you ever feel superior or inferior to others because of the way you speak? Is this right?

5 Who are you talking to or writing to?

Making language fit

Have you ever been told off because you didn't use the sort of language that an older person expected? Can you give an example?

In the following examples the wrong kind of language is used.

Scene 1: *Boy in bed. Mother is anxious.*

> How are you feeling, Jimmy love?

> The agony has abated Madam, thank you for your kind enquiry.

Scene 2: *Boss at desk. Office boy facing her.*

> I'm letting you have the afternoon off, but please see that you are in promptly tomorrow.

> Oh ta love! Be seeing you then!

Can you suggest what is more likely to have been said?

Mum/Mrs Green/Cllr Green

The kind of language we use often depends on how well we know people and how comfortable we feel with them. Look at these expressions:

1. Watcha mum!	2. Good morning, Mrs Green, do sit down.	3. On behalf of the Council may I welcome . . .
Morning all!	Good day to you!	I have the honour to introduce
Cheers!	Delighted to see you again!	It is my privilege to present . . .
See you!	It was a pleasure	We say a reluctant farewell to . . .
Take care!	Until we meet again – have a safe journey!	We wish every happiness to our colleague on her retirement . . .

G

1. You will see that the phrases in group 1 are used among close friends, members of a family, school children. How would you describe the language of groups 2 and 3?
(Cllr = Councillor, someone who serves on a local council.)

2. Think of some more greetings and decide which of the three groups they belong to.

3. Here are some expressions that belong to group 1, 2 or 3.

Put each one in the group to which it belongs.
Example
Group 1: She's a cocky so-and-so
Group 2: She is very conceited
Group 3: She has a greatly exaggerated opinion of herself

Now try with these expressions:
(a) I am feeling rather disappointed   I am as sick as a parrot
I must confess to being extremely disappointed
(b) It's a rip off   It's much too dear   The cost is exorbitant

Most of the time we change our language to suit the situation without realising it. For example, you probably use a different

kind of language with each of the following people:
1. Your family and school friends.
2. An adult you don't know very well.
3. Your head teacher.
How does your language change? What effect can it have if you use the wrong kind of language?

It is just the same when you are learning a foreign language. You have to learn not only what words *mean* but also which words are *suitable* for which situation. You can easily give the wrong impression, when speaking another language, by choosing the wrong words.

Inside knowledge

People in particular jobs often use words that outsiders do not understand – technical terms.

DOCTOR: I am afraid that you are suffering from general *coryza* and there is no treatment . . .

PATIENT: (*horrified*) Oh doctor, you don't mean . . !

DOCTOR: Yes, you have a cold.

Technical terms can be confusing to people who do not understand them. Are they necessary? Why is it important that everybody should agree about their exact meaning? What advantage is there in using these special words?

G Here are some technical terms that are used in connection with various activities. They have been jumbled up. Can you say which activities they are needed for? **a foot-fault; to cream; a selvedge; to baste; the alternator; offside; low-calorie content; the present tense; the accelerator; kerb-drill; top-spin; democracy; a glacier; square root; crochet; a T-square; a sweeper; a bully-off; a major scale.**

Take one *school subject* and list the new 'technical terms' (words used with a special meaning) that you have had to learn since you started it. In science you may have met the word 'solution'. You probably already knew the word meant the answer to a problem, but what does it mean in science?

When you have made your list of new words compare it with the lists of other groups. Put your lists together and make a dictionary of new words for each subject, to be used by new pupils coming to your school.

TIME TABLE

Monday	Tu
music	
Geography	
French	
P.E.	
Science	
Craft	
Maths	

Communicating

When we are using words to communicate we always have to start from what the person we are talking to or writing for already knows. How could you describe to someone who has been blind from birth the different colours of snooker balls? How could you explain to a deaf person what it is that you like about your favourite record?

People who are good at explaining things keep in mind what their listener knows already. Could you draw an animal you had never seen, but only heard described? That is what the German artist Albrecht Dürer (1471–1528) did. He got a letter and a sketch telling about a strange animal that nobody in Europe had seen before. From the information he was given he made this woodcut in the year 1515.

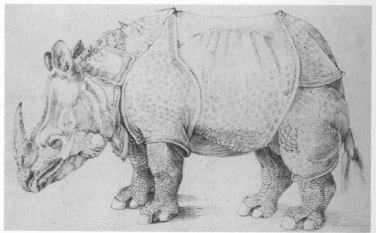

Here is a description of an *octopus* (written for adults). Rewrite it in language that an eight-year-old could understand without using a dictionary. (You may have to use *your* dictionary, though!) Remember that short sentences are easier to read and that the words you use must be simple.

The octopus is carnivorous, its diet consisting mainly of crabs. It has a beak with which it bites its prey, injecting it with a paralysing toxin. It can then carry the prey to its lair, usually a rocky crevice on the sea bed.

6 Bad language

Can language be 'bad'? It can if it doesn't do the job it is meant to do.

For instance *an instruction* that is hard to follow is bad language.

So is *a description* that doesn't give a clear picture.

The question to ask about language is: what is the speaker/writer trying to do with the words, and is the job done well?

Gobble-degook

Words can do their job badly if they are hard to understand. Official government language is often very complicated – it is jokingly known as 'gobbledegook'. The D.O.E. (Department of the Environment) – a government department – has been worried because the official forms that are sent out about things like payment of rates or rent allowances often use hard words when simpler words would do. The people who write the forms have now been asked to find easier words.

P Here are six examples of sentences used on forms. Try rewriting them more simply. Use a dictionary to avoid the words which are in italics and make any other changes you think are needed.

1. *Claimants* will find it *advantageous* to keep a detailed account of expenses at the time when they are *incurred*.

2. Payments will be *the equivalent* of the number of days lost.

3. Note that this travel warrant is for the *exclusive* use of the warrant holder.

4. The only *exceptions* to this rule will be for those *prevented* from applying through age or *infirmity*.

5. Earnings should be calculated *approximately* for the period *specified*.

6. Amount of tax will depend on the total income and on allowances *ultimately* claimed.

Compare your answers with those of others in your group and take a vote to decide which wording would be easiest to understand.

Spelling

Spelling in English used to vary a lot, before the invention of printing. Even in Shakespeare's time (1564–1616) writers did not always use the same spellings. Do you think it is important to be able to spell correctly? Why?

G 1. Discuss in your group the jobs for which accurate 'standard' spelling is especially important. (For example, suppose a doctor gets the spelling of a medicine wrong on a prescription form for the chemist, what might happen?)

2. If you are bad at spelling (and many people are) how can you help yourself?

3. Who decides in English how words should be spelled?

Too many 'fillers'

When we are talking – perhaps describing something that has happened – we all need to make pauses to give our brains time to find the next words we are looking for. To fill in the pauses we get into the habit of putting in 'filler' words, such as:

– sort of –   – well –
– actually –   – you know –

Some people may use so many of these filler words that we can't concentrate on what they are saying – we get bored.

G Try this experiment. Make a tape recording of someone in your group telling you about something that happened to her or him recently. Listen to the recordings each group has made and list the pauses and the fillers used.

When we write we don't use these fillers. Why not?

Thought-less words

It is not only the 'filler words' that we get tired of. Some expressions which once sounded fresh and interesting get used so often that they lose their force. Some are *similes* – saying one thing is like another.

Can you find more interesting ways of saying the following?

S 1. He went as red as a beetroot.

2. She turned white as a sheet.

3. The field was as flat as a pancake.

Some words or expressions become 'catch phrases' in common use. We use them to criticise someone without thinking exactly what it is we are trying to say. You may hear someone called a 'Commie' or a 'Fascist'. What do these words really mean?

1. Can you think of examples of catch phrases used by older people to describe younger people nowadays?
2. Do you or your friends use catch phrases to criticise older people or other groups of young people? Why is it a form of 'bad language' to use labels like this without thinking clearly what they mean?

One common kind of thoughtless expression is the *cliché*. (It is a French word meaning the block that the printer makes copies from. So the cliché is used like a rubber stamp, without stopping to think.)

Advertisements are often full of clichés. For example, holiday brochures speak of 'sun-drenched beaches'. Look at some holiday brochures and find more examples.

Many pop songs use clichés because it is not easy to find rhymes. You can guess the words that are coming because they are cliché words:
– I feel like dying', you've got me cr. . .'.
– I love you so, baby please don't . . .!
Write a pop song, using as many clichés as possible.

Other clichés are used because they sound impressive, although they often don't mean very much. Listen to people being interviewed on news programmes.
In this day and age . . .   To be perfectly honest . . .
At this moment in time . . .   That is the acid test.
Do you use clichés? Try to list them.

Another type of bad language (doing things with words but not doing it well) is the use of words that are not needed.
In each of the phrases below there is an unnecessary word or words. Can you pick them out?

1. His car is a red colour.
2. Don't over exaggerate.
3. Speaking personally, I myself think . . .
4. This is a new innovation.
5. An old, prehistoric monster.
6. At about 10 o'clock approximately.
7. Entry is limited to children under ten only.

Are there any expressions that you are tired of hearing, which you feel are used unthinkingly by, for example, disc jockeys, teachers, parents?

Advertising

Not all advertising is bad language. An advertisement does its job well if it persuades us to buy the product, but sometimes the language is dishonest. Exaggeration in advertising is a form of dishonesty.

On page 11 we looked at the commonest words used to advertise various products. Look again at some of those advertisements and pick out words that seem to you to be 'loaded': that is, they are intended to influence you to make you buy the thing that is advertised.

Here are some examples of loaded words:

The deep down secret of deep clean carpets.

Find other examples of 'loaded words' in advertisements.

Using language!

DON'T SWEAR DAMMIT!

In Wales you will sometimes hear this remark: 'He was using language!' It means he was using bad language. We have seen in this unit that there are lots of different kinds of bad language. But usually, 'bad language' means swearing. Why do we swear? Swearing can make language very boring. In most languages the swear words were originally 'taboo' words, that is words about the things we don't usually mention:

– fear of the unknown (death, damnation, the devil)
– the basic ways our bodies work

Using a taboo word relieves the speaker's feelings (of surprise, shock, fear etc.). Swearing may also cover up fear that we don't want others to notice. That is why people tend to swear when they are afraid and insecure. But swearing can become just a habit. As with other words, the 'taboo' words soon get worn out by too much use and lose their value. You can compare them with banknotes that get flimsy and worn by over-use and have to be replaced.

Here are some things for you to discuss in your group:
1. Do you ever swear? How often? What is your commonest swear word?
2. Are there some people you would not like to swear in front of? Why?
3. Are some swear words worse than others? If so, why?
4. Do your parents swear? How often?